France, European Defence and NATO

Karine Lisbonne-de Vergeron

Research Fellow at the Global Policy Institute,
London Metropolitan University, London

October 2008

About the Author

Karine Lisbonne-de Vergeron is a Research Fellow on defence at the Global Policy Institute. She is the author of *Contemporary Indian Views of Europe* (2006) and *Contemporary Chinese Views of Europe* (2007), jointly published by Chatham House and the Robert Schuman Foundation in English and French and is the co-author of *L'art avec pertes ou profit* published by Flammarion in 2007. She has previously specialised in international relations and European politics.

Contents

Foreword

France has long been the most ardent advocate of a stronger European defence identity and has set it as one of the priorities of its EU Presidency. The summer 2008 events in Georgia have reinforced France's case for a stronger more autonomous European defence capacity. The US inability to help its close ally has allowed Europe to take a leading role. Russia's determination has been seen by some 'as the last nail in the coffin of the unipolar world dream'. In the new multi-polar world order shaping up, the EU has emerged as an autonomous global diplomatic player. To consolidate its position, it must complement its unparalleled soft power with a credible autonomous defence capacity.

In the complex world we live in, Europe must use its distinctive history and voice to promote its values and interests. Its dialogue-based approach to conflict resolution, its expertise at negotiation and compromise could provide the best antidote to a Manichean conflictual view of the world, promoted by too many leaders, to the East, South and West. Europe has many diplomatic assets, not least its historical links with many parts of the world and its economic and social might and attractiveness, which should enable it to play the long game and to nurture its image as a honest broker.

But for Europe's voice to carry, not only unity will be required, as shown in the face of Russia, but also military clout. Whatever happens in the US election, however the EU/NATO relationship evolves, Europe will have to increasingly provide for its security and raise its defence expenditure. Faced with strict fiscal constraints and increasingly complex security challenges, European countries have carefully to consider the efficiency of their defence spending. They must do it in a collaborative and coherent way, as proposed by the French authorities.

In this booklet, Karine Lisbonne-de Vergeron, Research Fellow at the Global Policy Institute, provides an up-to-date insight into the official French views regarding the defence priorities of the country and their integration in existing European processes. She outlines and analyses French proposals for the future of European Security and Defence Policy (ESDP), based on the June 2008 French Defence White Paper, on the French EU presidency agenda and on interviews. These proposals, which take into account strategic as well as fiscal considerations, call for an updating of the 2003 European Security

Strategy, a renovation of the NATO/EU relationship and aim to increase the defence capabilities of the EU thanks to greater cooperation between countries through the pooling of assets and intelligence and increased industrial and research cooperation, among others. She also looks at how France and Britain, who together are responsible for the lion's share of European Defence spending, could further their military cooperation, either bi-laterally or within the framework of ESDP.

The Global Policy Institute is therefore very pleased to publish this timely report. It should be read by anyone with an interest in European Defence, as it raises many strategic and industrial issues, which European countries all have to face, and none more than the UK.

Jacques Reland
Head of European Research
Global Policy Institute, London
October 2008

Preface

The no vote of June 2008 to the Lisbon Treaty in Ireland, the only European Union (EU) member state to have put it to a referendum, halted the expectations, and the hopes, that it could be ratified by the end of that year. With some 53% of Irish voters rejecting the Treaty, the result has triggered a renewed round of reflection, re-assessment and recrimination about the processes and purpose of the EU, not only in Ireland but also more widely. This may well be a defining moment for the international rule of law and democracy which the EU pioneers in the world. One consequence is already clear: if the people of Europe are to follow their political establishments towards 'ever closer union', changes of process, however necessary, must be explained and justified in terms of promoting policies which Europeans can see serve their interests and address their concerns. In other words, Europe must become more political.

Defence is undoubtedly one such policy area. Traditions of neutrality amongst six (including Ireland) of the 27 Member States of the EU notwithstanding, all opinion polls show that greater military co-operation is supported by most Europeans. According to Eurobarometer polls in 2007, 67% of European citizens support a more integrated defence and foreign policy at the European level. On defence in particular, 75% support the common European and defence policy. Even in supposedly eurosceptical Britain, 57% of the public are favourable[1]. Perhaps yet more telling, around some 80% of EU citizens, including Britons, are in favour of Europe having the ability to decide upon deploying forces without the support of the United States[2]. Security is also a growing concern with more than 80% of the European public wishing to see the fight against terrorism jointly managed at a European, as well as at a national level.

So, how might this be achieved? Recent developments in French defence and foreign policy suggest two significant steps forward, both in the short and the medium term. First, it is clear that France's new President, Nicolas Sarkozy, is determined to make the development of the European Security and Defence Policy (ESDP) a priority of the French presidency of the European Union during the second half of 2008. Second, France has signalled the possibility of fully rejoining the military command structure of the North Atlantic Treaty Organisation (NATO) whilst progressing both beforehand, and in tandem, a strengthening of specifically European defence. The aim would be to encourage a renewal of NATO, through both a clarification of its relationship with the EU and a clarification of the responsibilities of its European member states, these being possibly the subject of a reassessment which could take place at the 60th anniversary summit of the Alliance in April 2009.

European defence in the form of ESDP also has a forthcoming anniversary: its 10th, at the end of 2008. Arguably, since 1998 when it was initiated, much progress has been made both in institutional and in operational terms. The EU has, to date, successfully conducted some 17 civilian-military external operations. Despite the significance of such developments, it is widely accepted that the resources allocated to achieve them are not enough to provide Europe with a modern, fully effective, rapid reaction and projection force. Moreover, the increasingly unstable international context in which Europe now finds itself makes remedying these deficiencies all the more pressing. As new powers emerge, as the centre of gravity of the world economy shifts from the West to Asia and as new issues, such as climate change, arise to complicate existing ideological, ethnic and cultural fault-lines, the EU will increasingly have to apply itself to the task of promoting a more stable international order[3].

Traditionally, a key stumbling block of European defence development has been the longstanding fear in some countries, particularly in Britain and in those Member States formerly in the Soviet bloc, that the EU and NATO are inevitably competing, rather than co-operating institutions. France's position outside the integrated command has fostered a certain degree of suspicion that the true object of her European ambition in defence was to detach Europe from the United States strategically, an outcome deemed unwelcome either because it would imply an unacceptable further political integration of the EU, or an unacceptable weakening of European defence towards a still possibly dangerous Russia. Such notions have been on occasion encouraged, it must be said, by some influential circles in the United States.

President Sarkozy seems determined to create a stronger and more harmonious transatlantic relationship which could allow France to rejoin the military command structure of the Alliance, having fostered a stronger and more coherent EU defence posture under her Presidency of the EU. This could constitute a significant opportunity to change these misperceptions and make good these deficiencies. He has matched his diplomacy with the United States with a significant approach to Britain: his successful state visit to London on 27 March 2008 paved the way for a renewed cooperation between the two Member States which are the main providers of troops and the largest producers and buyers of military hardware of the European Union. Ten years after the Saint-Malo accord between the two countries, defence seems to offer perhaps the best prospect of new bi-lateral initiatives.

Indeed, as France reviewed her own defence and security strategy in the White Paper published on 18 June 2008 and as she took on the Presidency of the European Union on 1 July 2008 for a six months period, it was expected that she would underline her intention to develop European defence in four main areas: first, by evolving her relationship with the United States in particular with regard to her relationship with NATO, second by harnessing this to the creation of a specifically European defence capability, third by ensuring that this, in turn, is reflected in the development of her own defence capabilities, fourth by ensuring that all these goals are expressed in her diplomacy on defence within the EU during her Presidency of the Union and beyond, both at EU level and with particular partners, notably Britain.

1. A new transatlantic strategic outlook: France and the United States

When Nicolas Sarkozy came into office as French President in May 2007, the twin questions of France's position in Europe and of her relationship with the United States loomed very large. The 2005 rejection of the then proposed Constitutional Treaty, regardless of the precise factors which led to that result, had struck at the very core of France's European commitment and confidence. The rift between Washington and Paris over the war in Iraq, regardless of the perceived vindication of French caution by subsequent events, was also deep. In his first major foreign policy speech the French President set out his belief that the construction of Europe remains an absolute priority for France. In November 2007, by his first state visit to Washington, he sought to transcend the difficulties in the Franco-American relationship.

Speaking before the joint session of Congress on 7 November 2007, he drew a line under past strains by signalling his eagerness to renew the friendship and the long-standing alliance between the two countries. This shift reflected a strategic sense that a new feeling of trust was required between the United States and Europe, in particular that the interests of the West demanded a strong trans-Atlantic alliance and thus that the interests of the United States demanded a strong Europe. This ambition is particularly significant in the realm of defence and plays directly to the new consensus in Washington that the United States is operating at or near her limit of military capability[4]. Based on the pragmatic assessment that there are more crises likely to emerge than there are currently the means to face them, the French President underlined his conviction that the United States should have a clear vested 'strategic interest in a Europe that can assert itself as a strong and credible security partner'[5]. Rather than exploit the United States's new found vulnerability after the failures and disappointments of her occupation of Iraq, he reaffirmed the Franco-American partnership in the hope of re-engaging the United States in the process of European Union integration.

2. France and NATO

The main indicator of France's diplomatic shift is the offer that she could soon fully return to NATO's military command structure. Since August 2007, Sarkozy has called for 'the renovation of NATO and of its relationship with France'[6]. He has also signalled his desire for France to play a renewed role within the Alliance and in Washington asserted his wish to see an improvement in EU-NATO cooperation. Arguably, to date, France's NATO participation has been far from limited. Some 4,000 French military personnel are currently involved in NATO-led operations and more than 7,000 soldiers are anticipated be put on alert as part of the NATO Response Force (NRF) in addition to air, naval and command capabilities. Since the last French defence White paper in 1994, France's presence has been further expanded, in particular through the 1995 decision to attend the Alliance's defence ministerial meetings. France, however, remains absent from the defence planning committee as well as from the permanent chain of command.

The re-integration case

What is really significant is that Sarkozy's initiative undoubtedly broached a subject which had long been 'a taboo'[7]. Hitherto, the issue of France's status in the Alliance – a legacy of the decision made by President Charles de Gaulle in March 1966 to withdraw from the integrated military structure of NATO[8] – and its relationship with the ESDP had been perceived by some of France's European partners as competing with NATO. France's new relationship with the United States should transform this reasoning and certainly opens up the possibility of a dramatic improvement in EU-NATO cooperation.

Such a move is definitely a very serious initiative[9]. Of crucial significance in the long-term analysis of France's position towards NATO and the ESDP is the fact that the new so-called *Livre Blanc* on defence, unveiled on 18 June 2008 (which is valid for the next fifteen years), considers that 'a new rapprochement with the command structure of NATO' should be consistent with respecting the essential principles of French defence policy initially established by de Gaulle, above all the continuing complete strategic, technological and operational independence of France's nuclear forces. The White Paper recalls that France retains full freedom of strategic assessment and deployment, and in particular that no military forces will be permanently placed under NATO's command in peacetime. This new 'integrated' participation in NATO will not entail an automatic contribution to NATO's military interventions[10]. It derives from the conviction that France's present strategic posture lacks clarity and must change in order to reinforce her goal of progress towards an enhanced European security and defence policy[11]. The French President had explained already in August 2007 that the prospect of France 'playing a full role' in NATO should be understood as going 'hand in hand' with the development of 'an independent European defence'.

These were themes to which Sarkozy returned in his address to the US Congress, when he laid great emphasis on the need for the EU and NATO to complement each other. Indeed, a key aspect of France's commitment to NATO is her determination to improve the Alliance's co-operation with the EU. This should be built on the growing recognition by the United States of the strategic, operational and functional complementarities between the two organisations. After all, 21 of NATO's 26 members are currently in the EU, all of which, apart from Denmark, are also in the ESDP. This is also underlined by the positive impact that France's strengthened involvement in NATO could have on the process of renovating the Alliance, in particular with respect to streamlining its organisation[12].

Towards a renovated NATO?
It is likely that France will formally decide upon its full return to the command structure at the NATO's 60th

anniversary summit, which will be jointly held in France and in Germany in the spring of 2009, a few months after the end of the French Presidency of the EU. According to the new French White Paper, this Summit should be the occasion to launch a debate on the renovation of NATO's present structures. In many respects, the Alliance is still very far from coming to terms with the abrupt shift of emphasis away from focusing purely on territorial defence in Europe which followed the 9/11 terrorist outrage. The 2002 Prague NATO Summit committed the Alliance 'to meet the challenges to the security of (its) forces, populations, territory, from wherever they may come'[13]. In August 2003, the International Security and Assistance Force (ISAF) in Afghanistan was launched, the first such NATO military intervention outside the so-called Euro-Atlantic area. Yet, this transformation of role has given rise to intractable difficulties and debates, notably on mission definition and on the lack of assets required for operations. Afghanistan presents great challenges to the Alliance. There are challenges too on enlargement, as was evidenced at the 59th Summit in 2008, held in Bucharest, over the debate on Georgia and Ukraine's position with regards to the Alliance. NATO, however, did decide formally to extend an invitation to Albania and Croatia to join the Alliance, a move which would bring the organisation to a total of 28 members.

In this context, the French White Paper released in June 2008 suggested three main goals to consider in a so-called 'renovation' of NATO. First, it underlined the need to streamline NATO's command and planning structures.

Second, it suggested the launch of a further assessment of new security threats to be taken into account in the Alliance's mission. Third, and in the context of a renewed transatlantic link, it proposed the definition of a better responsibility-sharing and equilibrium between Americans and Europeans within NATO. Such a proposal is likely to be welcomed by France's traditionally more Atlanticist European partners and in particular by Britain.

3. EU-NATO complementarity

Achieving EU-NATO complementarity will require first and foremost the rejection of any of the old temptations to define an *a priori* strict distribution of tasks between NATO and the EU. Key to this is the shift towards an explicit complementarity between the two institutions based on what each of them are best able to achieve in any given situation. The French White Paper thus calls for a 'renovated strategic partnership between Europe and the United States of America' leading to an improvement in EU-NATO cooperation. Of particular significance is the fact that this formulation has found a positive echo from American sources. As *The Economist* predicted, in a recent article, 'one obstacle to more joint European defence – American objections to a potential rival to NATO – has been removed'[14]. On 25 February 2008,

Victoria Nuland, the American Ambassador to NATO, in a speech in London[15], welcomed France's proposal by acknowledging that the United States 'needs a stronger EU', that Europe needs a capacity to act independently and that America 'needs a Europe that is able and willing to do so'. She went on: 'In Paris, we have a President who is prepared to use his EU presidency to strengthen Europe's defence contribution and then bring France back into a renovated NATO. In Washington, leaders of all stripes are calling for more, not less Europe. And in London, David Miliband is calling on us to support the global "civilian surge" for democracy with both soft and hard power'[16]. As one commentator observed, such a move has been 'widely and rightly welcomed' since it offers an end to the arguments over European defence between France and NATO's other two important military powers, the United States and Britain[17].

Washington's enthusiasm has been further fostered by Sarkozy's decision in April 2008 at the NATO Summit in Bucharest, to send more French troops to Afghanistan at a time when this mission is considered, by the United States, as the most pressing task on NATO's agenda. France has further committed 700 soldiers who have been deployed (at some cost in lives already) in the North-East of Kabul in the Kapisa province to reinforce its contribution and presence there[18]. This apparent new American recognition for improved independent European defence capacities and the need for a complementary between NATO and ESDP is likely to increase following the US presidential elections in November 2008 since many

European and American experts believe that it is in line with the strategic thinking of both Senators John McCain and Barack Obama.

In operational terms, the Alliance should be interested in stronger European military capabilities that satisfy transatlantic demands for better burden-sharing. NATO has already some 48,350 soldiers currently deployed in Afghanistan and more than 13,000 operating in the Balkans. Given this present logistical and military burden, there is likely to be a number of crises where NATO will not want to conduct operations and where Europe, with a reinforced military capability and without any duplication with NATO, would be able to do so. Already this has happened in the case of the Democratic Republic of Congo with the deployment of the ESDP operation EUFOR Artemis in 2003 following the unrest in Ituri. The deployment of 2,000 men, of whom 1,700 were French with the Swedes supplying the second-largest contingent, was successful. Nevertheless, it demonstrated the need to develop new European defence concepts for preventive deterrence in the form of operational and logistical capabilities such as joint battlegroups and rapid response forces (See below, section 4).

The EU intervention in the Balkans may also be far from over. Should a further crisis emerge in Kosovo or in Macedonia, Europe must be able to act decisively to keep the peace. Arguably, the creation of the ESDP in 1999 was as a direct result of the European lack of power during the tragic Balkans wars of the previous decade. Today of the 15,000 troops of the NATO-led operations in the Balkans, some 11,000 are from European countries. In the framework of the ESDP, operations there presently include notably the EUFOR-Althea military presence in Bosnia-Herzegovina since December 2004 (taking over from the then NATO force) as well as the EU Police Mission which has been deployed since January 2003. Furthermore, following events in Georgia, the EU may have to envisage the possibility of other crises adjacent to its borders, perhaps in Ukraine, Moldova or Belarus.

The consideration that NATO and ESDP are complementary rather than competitors is therefore based on a geopolitical fact: some countries, in particular in sub-Saharan Africa but also in the Middle East, are more likely to request European rather than NATO assistance for political or historical reasons[19]. The European force in Chad, which is currently operating with 3,000 soldiers already deployed under the command of the Irish Lieutenant-General Nash, is further evidence for this. Military experts agree that the governments of Chad and of the Central African Republic more generally 'would never have accepted NATO's intervention to help resolve the Darfur crisis'[20]. There is also the diverging natures of the EU and NATO. It is widely acknowledged that, unlike the military alliance that NATO represents, the European Union is able to build jointly on the civil and the military aspects of crisis management. Therefore, given the strategic significance of ensuring regional stability, European-led operations could be operative in some theatres, notably Africa, where NATO forces would not be engaged[21]. This will require however an efficient and effective relationship between NATO and the EU, which, in turn, entails a stronger European defence. For NATO and the EU to be in a position fully to cooperate on defence will also include at some point allaying Turkey's concerns, which have hitherto blocked much formal contact between the two organisations[22].

4. The development
of European defence

Overall, demands for European military and combined civil and military capabilities are increasing. This is made all the more evident since the United Nations obviously does not have its own troops for peace-keeping operations and because, as underlined above, the Alliance cannot be involved in all crisis theatres. At present there are Member States of the EU taking part in some 33 external operations, 12 of which are under the ESDP framework[23]. Nonetheless, France's assessment is that 'there is no excess but rather a shortage of capabilities in Europe'[24]. This view is also shared by Britain and indeed more widely within and outside Europe. In his first major speech on Europe in November 2007, the British Foreign Secretary, David Miliband, underlined that 'European member states must improve their capabilities' and 'must be able to deploy soft and hard power to promote democracy and tackle conflict beyond its borders'[25].

Since its formal creation in June 1999 at the Cologne European Council, there can be no doubt that the ESDP has made significant progress. In particular, it has been incrementally institutionalised through the subsequent creation of the so-called Political and Security Committee, the Military Committee, the Military staff and in June 2000 the civilian dimension of the ESDP was launched. 'A Civil Military Cell' within the EU military staff was further set up in 2005 following the December 2004 European Council decision. Its main goal is to liaise between the EU's civil and military bodies on issues related to crisis management and prevention but it was also tasked with setting up the operations centre – which is not a standing, fully-manned headquarters – principally for civilian-military operations carried out autonomously by the EU and when no national operation headquarters is identified[26].

The adoption of the first European Security Strategy in December 2003 further provided the EU with a necessary political framework for ESDP in line with its global role. It established three fundamental objectives to promote European values and defend Europe's security: first, the use of a combination of civilian ('soft power') and military capabilities, second, the promotion of effective multilateralism by defending and developing international law and third, to build security in the 'European neighbourhood', of crucial importance by acting particularly, in the Balkans and in the Middle East[27].

Since 2004, the European Defence Agency has been successfully established, giving the EU a much-needed framework for a long-term policy to help EU member states improve their defence capabilities for crisis-management operations under ESDP through a global approach and to strengthen the European defence industrial base. Furthermore, the battlegroups which were jointly proposed in February 2004, by Britain, France and Germany after the success of the 2003 Artemis operation in the Democratic Republic of Congo have reinforced European rapid response capability[28]. Although two, out of a pool of fifteen, battlegroups are on permanent call for a period of six months[29] since January 2007, some doubts have emerged over their rapid deployability since none has yet been actually sent on missions. There are also concerns over the shortfalls in military capability, in particular concerning strategic air transport.

Moreover, the case for supporting inter-European industries has generally become stronger, especially given the United States' substantial technological superiority[30]. In 2006, defence expenditures accounted for 1.78% of the total GDP of the 26 EU Member States who are part of the European Defence Agency as against a ratio of 4.7% for the United States. Whilst new competition has emerged on a number of defence armament programmes from countries such as, for example, Israël, in Europe they have generally stagnated and are currently anticipated to trend lower. By contrast, around the world, military expenditures are increasing and amounted to some $1,200 billion in 2007. The US defence budget is about twice as large as that of all European defence budgets combined, with some 30% of it is allocated to investment compared to only 20% in Europe[31]. This decrease in European defence expenditure since the end of the Cold War has had a direct effect on much-needed investment in research and technology. In this, the United States further outspends Europe by more than six to one according to the European Commission's defence report issued in December 2007. Research and development in Europe is fragmented, leading to a serious wastage of scarce resources[32]. Military expenditure also varies across the EU. Whilst defence production is mainly concentrated in six member states (Germany, France, Britain, Italy, Spain and Sweden), which together account for more than 95% of military research and development expenditures[33], there is widespread duplication of programmes between member states, for example the development of 89 separate weapons systems in Europe compared to only 27 in the United States, or, despite lower budget expenditure, of three times more land armament systems programmes currently underway in Europe than in the United States[34]. This inevitably leads to unhelpful competition.

According to a 2005 study from the European Commission, the direct and indirect cost of obstacles to intra-community transfers amounts to some €3 billion per year[35]. At present, exports within the EU are dealt with in the same manner as exports to third countries[36]. The export of defence-related products, be it completed military equipment or spare parts, is also subject to national licensing schemes, not to mention the obstacles arising from national economic interests. The fragmentation imposed by 27 separate licensing frameworks also entails a significant administrative burden on companies, which impedes industrial competitiveness and appears to 'be out of proportion with actual control needs' since license application for intra-Community transfers are hardly ever rejected[37]. Improving the conditions for such cross-border transfers and trade should therefore be considered as key to fostering a more viable and competitive defence industrial base in Europe.

It is further acknowledged that isolated individual national defence budgets cannot finance the development of a full range of top quality products to maintain the necessary comprehensive and competitive technological and industrial base, especially given the increasing cost of military equipment. This is particularly true since the restructuring of armed forces in Europe is making the drive to improve competitiveness even greater. On 9 April 2008, the EU governments agreed that the European Defence Agency should produce a strategy in order to 'help meet future military needs, ensure inter-operability and standardization and share the ever-increasing cost of developing and procuring high-technology defence equipment'[38]. Indeed, the reinforcement of European capabilities and the creation of a proper internal market for arms and defence industries, through streamlining operational assets and pooling the costs of new military programmes or updates, are essential drivers of a strengthened European defence that will be sufficient to secure the EU's strategic independence of action. Such strengthened cooperation will also undoubtedly foster a more effective spending policy and therefore could ultimately deliver 'further savings to the taxpayer'[39].

As the EU will, in the future, increasingly have to develop more capabilities for external projection, including civilian and policing assets, providing these should nonetheless require harmonising the financial efforts made by individual European Member States on defence. This point was emphasised by the French President in August 2007. However, given the fact that military budgets in Europe are going down in relative terms, it must inevitably be seen as a long-term aspiration. At present, between half and two-thirds of European spending on defence and security, depending on which measurements are used, comes from Britain and France.

5. The new French defence and national security policy

The last French White Paper on defence was undertaken in the aftermath of the Cold War in 1994[40], before the creation of the European Security and Defence Policy. The new one offers a radical change of approach for a more assertive French defence and national security policy as well as a significant framework to set out both the national and international context in which France's defence ambitions will evolve over the next fifteen years.

So, what does it mean for France's defence policy?
Whilst reappraising France's security environment, it makes strong commitments in pursuit of improved national capabilities, through far-reaching reforms of the military and security forces. Taking into account the greater security threats and the emergence of a more

unstable international environment, including terrorism, national security is redefined to include five key functions: knowledge and anticipation, prevention, deterrence, protection and intervention. In this, knowledge and anticipation becomes a new strategic axis of French policy and its first line of defence to guarantee its autonomy in decision-making and to ensure the country's strategic initiative.

Of particular significance at a national level is the assessment that[41]:

1. There should be a shift of focus from France's historic spheres towards a 'strategic arc' of instability that stretches from the Atlantic to the Mediterranean, the Arab-Persian Gulf and the Indian Ocean where the risks relating to the strategic interests of both France and Europe are considered the most acute. This is in line with the announcement in January 2008 of the creation of a new French military base at Abu Dhabi, her first in the Gulf.

2. The growing importance of Asia and the prospect of major conflicts emerging in this region should be taken into account given the implications this would have for France's and Europe's security.

3. France should make a very substantial change in the system of defence and military cooperation agreements she presently holds in Africa. The goal set out by the White Paper is to evolve towards a partnership between Europe and Africa and a greater

cooperation in defence and security to enhance the development of African peace-keeping capabilities[42].

At a national level, the radical change stems from the new format of the French armed forces, which in future will be determined on the basis of operational goals and needs, giving France a proposed ground force of 88,000 soldiers and a joint fleet of 300 combat aircraft. This will allow an estimated necessary force projection capability of 70 combat aircraft and 30,000 soldiers able to be deployed with six months notice for a period of at least a year and 5,000 soldiers and 10 combat aircraft on permanent alert. French decision-making and planning structures will also be modified with the creation of a defence and national security council as well as of a national intelligence council and a national intelligence advisor[43]. Defence spending should increase by one percentage point above inflation from 2012 with capital spending for procurement increasing from € 15 billion to € 18 billion on average per year from 2009 to 2020. In time, the result should be an army which is better equipped to respond to new threats and risks including terrorism and cyber-attacks.

France's long-term European perspective
Making the European Union a major player in crisis management and in international security lies at the heart of France's new defence and security policy over the next fifteen years[44]. The White Paper sets out, in particular, an analysis of the need for greater projection forces and advocates that priority should be given to constitute effectively European intervention capabilities

of 60,000 soldiers complemented by the necessary air and naval support (see below, section 6). The EU should also aim to have the capabilities required to plan for and deploy two or three peace-keeping or peace-enforcement operations and several civilian operations of lesser scope in separate conflict zones.

Especially noteworthy are also the following further proposed developments in policy areas[45]:

1. The pooling of assets of several European countries to compensate for the lack of deployable forces in remote theatres of operation. For example, strategic and tactical transport, as well as in-flight refuelling aircraft[46] could be shared, as could further assets, notably Franco-British ones, in the field of air-mobile capabilities, such as helicopters[47], or in the field of naval-air capabilities, in particular through the association of aircraft carriers or on-board air units. This should be complemented by providing greater civil crisis management resources, including policing and judicial assets and by strengthening the role of the reserve forces for such deployments.

2. In the long term, the present funding concept for external operations could be replaced by a new procedure based upon the principle of financial solidarity amongst the Member States – those countries which will not contribute in operational terms to EU interventions abroad would instead contribute financially. Indeed, at present those member states that are most heavily involved in operations, be it in terms

of military equipment or in terms of soldiers deployed, are penalised by also carrying the financial burden that such commitment entails.

3. Increasing anticipation and analysis capabilities by a greater pooling of operational and background intelligence. In this context, it is suggested that themes of general interest could be jointly identified and unclassified information gathered from satellite surveillance shared.

4. These ambitions should be complemented by supporting the creation of an exchange and training programme for security and defence personnel between EU Member States and the establishment of a permanent European crisis management training centre.

5. Reinforcing the protection of European citizens, especially with regard to improving EU-wide cooperation in the fight against terrorism and organised crime. Of particular note is the suggestion that France will favour the creation of a European operational centre for civil protection and promote the establishment of a European college for civil security.

6. Reinforcing security and defence research and industrial cooperation in Europe. This should include in particular the three following directions: pursuing a joint analysis of military requirements, defining joint rules for defence procurement and reinforcing the action of the European Defence Agency. Setting out

France's industrial and technological priorities for 2025, the White paper further identifies four notable areas where concrete progress could be sought at a European level (though a start may be made on a purely bilateral or trilateral basis):

- First, in the field of aeronautic systems. As fighter aircraft programmes are reduced in scope, most European actors in this industry will have to tackle the need to update their competencies. The White Paper thus supports the inception of a European military aircraft manufacturer able to design future combat systems, both manned and unmanned.

- Second, in the field of land systems, the emergence of an integrated European industrial capability for land equipment.

- Third, in the field of electronic components, the objective should be to develop a European approach to preclude any situation of critical dependency on sources outside the EU.

- Fourth, although France will retain a national design and production capability for nuclear submarines, conventional submarines and surface ships could be opened up to European cooperation.

Above all, the harmonisation of military procurement needs between different Member States will be key to a greater streamlining of the European defence industry.

7. Enhancing European planning and command capability in particular with an independent standing strategic planning capacity (see below, section 7).

8. Initiating a European white paper on defence and security in agreement with France's EU partners. This could include a joint analysis of present and foreseeable threats as well as a definition of common European-wide security interests. It could also include a doctrinal framework for external intervention and for the use of force as well as a communication strategy on EU defence policy directed towards European citizens.

This analysis for a greater cooperation in the realm of European defence is put forward as a long-term perspective. It provides a fruitful context in which to consider how European defence could be reinforced. Moreover, a limited number of these proposals are likely to be part of the defence agenda which France may seek to put forward during her Presidency of the Union – notably the sharing of some assets, the enhancement of European defence capabilities or the development of European military training programmes.

6. The priority of defence in the French Presidency of the EU

France took over the Presidency of the EU at a very challenging time on account of the Irish 'no' vote to the Lisbon Treaty. This has put a halt – at least until, at the very earliest, the beginning of 2009, should a way forward be found to tackle the ratification issue – to a number of significant provisions in the Treaty on defence. These include the enhanced role of the EU's High Representative for external affairs, which would strengthen the long-term development of external and defence policy and the provision to allow Member States, who are willing to do so, to participate in the framework of permanent structured cooperation[48]. Nevertheless, the French President confirmed that he will stick to his intention to develop European defence over the French Presidency. In this, it is significant that on 2 July, the

British Foreign Secretary lent his support to Sarkozy's proposals on European defence, stressing that Europe must develop its military capabilities[49]. It is likely that France might concentrate in particular on the following areas: enhancing capabilities, updating the European security strategy, promoting NATO-ESDP cooperation.

In his speech on 17 June 2008 on national security and defence, the French President emphasised that 'there is only one way forward' which is to 'foster the European armament market, to stimulate cooperation so as to favour the creation of European companies which can compete at an international level and to encourage exports, whilst respecting international laws and ethical responsibility'[50]. Progress could therefore be sought in new commitments including the streamlining of existing capabilities as well as much-needed greater interoperability. Enhancing capability will thus most probably be a key defence priority of France's EU presidency. Some agreement could be achieved in particular towards the pooling of some naval and air assets. This might include the development of an air and sea group, based on a closer cooperation between Britain and France and allowing eventually for a French or a British aircraft carrier to be permanently at sea and which could benefit from European support such as frigates or refuelling tankers[51]. Crucial to this will be an agreement not only on the principle but also on the necessary modalities to do so, in particular between Britain and France.

Of significance also would be the possibility to ensure strengthened projection capabilities, in particular the development of a common fleet of military transport aircraft based around the future Airbus A400M as well as, air-mobile capabilities, such as helicopters (see below, section 7). Further initiatives might also include reinforcing space observation by building on the European system of satellite surveillance, and improving crisis management capabilities, for example concerning the evacuation of European citizens from crisis-affected areas. Strengthening and restructuring the European defence industry, taking into account all these factors will, however, inevitably require at least a medium-term perspective. Nevertheless, by launching some concrete initiatives and laying down the basis for greater cooperation in this field, the French Presidency could mark a key step towards creating much-needed substantial developments in European defence capabilities.

The decision at the December 1999 European Council in Helsinki to give the EU a military capability target, known as the Headline Goal, provided that the EU member states should be able to deploy a total of 60,000 soldiers within 60 days sustainable for a year. In this context, it is significant that Sarkozy reasserted, on 17 June 2008, the need for Europe really to be able to deploy such forces simultaneously in several distant theatres, and not only for one large military operation. Further initiatives along these lines should include defining guidelines for a combination of military and civilian operations of smaller scale, which could be conducted at the same time[52]. This should also be complemented with the proposal to foster the training of military officers through exchange programs[53], such as a 'military Erasmus'.

In his August 2007 speech, the French President also highlighted the need to update the current European common security strategy, adopted in 2003, to reflect the new geopolitical challenges and risks that Europe will have to face as well as the evolution of the EU itself. Indeed, since 2003, Europe has integrated further: the European Union has enlarged to 27 Member States, the European Defence Agency has come into being and the Schengen area has widened to embrace 24 nations since December 2007. At the same time, since 2003, new threats have emerged, in particular the proliferation of nuclear weapons, cyber-attacks, energy, water and food security, arms trafficking and space security. It is widely understood that this has been well received by France's European partners. The European outlook animating the proposals and the analysis put forward by the French White Paper on defence (see above, section 5) might also provide a useful basis for such an update. In this context, it is anticipated that the current examination of the European security strategy led by the Secretary General of the European Council, Javier Solana, with 'a view to proposing elements on how to improve the implementation and, as appropriate, elements to complement it'[54] could be adopted by the European Council in December 2008.

France could also seek during her Presidency of the EU to foster a better relationship between NATO and European defence by highlighting the complementarity between the two organisations. Further initiatives could include that of improving the strategic and operational planning capability of ESDP (see below, section 7).

Certainly, the French Presidency is determined to implement concrete achievements on defence and to set out a longer-term path for greater developments of capabilities. In this, France's new relationship with the United States may well provide the chance also for closer cooperation with Britain.

7. Franco-British cooperation and European defence

France and Britain are, of course, the key pillars of European defence, the only two nuclear powers in Europe, the sole EU members of the UN Security Council and the two EU member states with truly serious strategic capabilities. They have a strong claim to have been the originators of the European Security and Defence Policy during the December 1998 Saint-Malo Summit between the then French President, Jacques Chirac, and the British Prime Minister, Tony Blair. Ten years on, the state visit of the French President to the United Kingdom on 27 March 2008 paved the way for greater cooperation[55].

In anticipation of the French Presidency of the EU and drawing on the need to strengthen the ESDP, the two countries committed themselves to the development of new European military capabilities, which would simultaneously be available to NATO, in particular in the field of carrier group operations and helicopters. France and Britain further agreed to enhance the development of a combined maritime strike force which could be expanded to include other European countries able and willing to take part. European strategic lift capacity could also be enhanced by the coming into service of the military transport aircraft A400M and in particular by the Franco-British agreement 'to pursue a common approach in service support for interoperability and through life cycle costs optimisation, including common configuration management with other A400M nations' with the aim of covering the requirements of both France and Britain in a single joint contract[56]. They also agreed to give a new impetus to bilateral industrial defence cooperation in particular by increasing joint research and development efforts as well as by establishing measures to facilitate transfers between French and British companies.

Another area of cooperation includes Africa, notably through support to the African Standby Force for peace-keeping operations as well as in conjunction with other European partners and within the framework of the Euro-RECAMP programme. The two countries also committed themselves to allow for qualified civilians to be available for post-conflict stabilisation under the EU civilian headlines goal 2010 target[57]. In his speech on 2 July, the British Foreign Secretary further underlined his support for the French President's 'call for the EU to play a greater role in crisis management.'[58]

Could such moves mark the start of a geopolitically significant 'entente formidable' between the two key nations for European defence? British and French visions of Europe's need to become an 'open, outward looking and global actor'[59] are certainly now converging. So what would be needed? Two points seem central. First, there needs to be a combination of greater defence capacities. Second, Britain and France should agree on common orientations. As Alastair Cameron, head of the European security programme of the Royal United Services Institute puts it, 'with the emphasis of the (bilateral) summit having been on practical issues – such as the helicopter initiative or the announcement of a joint defence R&D investment' – the premise of this new Franco-British rapprochement 'looks very good indeed for Europe. With both countries reaching a common understanding that deployable and therefore real defence capabilities are those currently required, ESDP could indeed undergo significant development'[60].

For European defence to be taken forward will require France and Britain to continue and deepen the collaboration which has been a feature of 2007-2008. A number of controversial questions, however, remain unresolved, notably the details of a new institutional framework for NATO and ESDP, important procurement questions and whether an agreement can be reached for the setting up of a permanent strategic planning structure for the EU. This last point would seek to reinforce Europe's ability to anticipate crises and plan operational needs avoiding any forms of duplication with the existing NATO Supreme Headquarters Allied Powers Europe. Up until now, Britain has voiced its reluctance to support such a move, on the well-worn grounds that it would only create further bureaucracy and could impede NATO's existing capabilities. It is significant, however, that these ideas seem to enjoy support in Washington. Indeed, it appears that 'American diplomats have spoken privately to their UK counterparts making the case for a compromise'[61]. According to Karl-Heinz Kamp, director of the research division of the NATO Defence College: 'Gone are the days when the then US representative to NATO, Ambassador Nicholas Burns, characterized the EU attempts to build up an independent military planning cell as "the greatest threat for the future of the Alliance". Instead, every successful step taken by the European Union to strengthen its military capacities is welcomed by Washington as an improvement for Euro-Atlantic capabilities in general.'[62]

Given the present international strategic context and the clear need for Europe to cope with an increasing number of crises, creating a small independent standing strategic and operational planning capability would specifically increase the efficiency to plan in advance – i.e. before a decision of the European Council – possible external operations of both a civil and military nature. As a general proposition, these ideas are supported by many EU member states. It is clear that European planning capabilities need improvement. An accord between Britain and France on this issue would contribute significantly to the strengthening of European defence. It will also require political will. Without doubt, France's willingness to rejoin NATO fully, as part of the strengthening of European defence, offers a unique opportunity for closer cooperation.

Conclusion

The democratic challenge set by the failure of the old Constitutional Treaty, and now the uncertainty over whether the Lisbon Treaty can be ratified, is all too real. One test for European defence initiatives will be, therefore, whether they can engage with the European electorate and create a continent-wide sense of shared security interests which require really serious shared solutions. In some respects, the opportunities for this at present are substantial. Rising energy and food costs are uppermost in citizens' minds across the Union. The growing sense of economic vulnerability is giving a new saliency and urgency to the idea that Europeans should be standing together militarily in a way not seen, perhaps, since the Cold War.

Furthermore, progress in the Union often comes in the

face of adversity. The Irish rejection of the Lisbon Treaty might actually strengthen France's hand under her Presidency of the EU, not weaken it, because it could provide a more receptive audience of European politicians anxious to prove that they can address substantive issues and promote policies that are of strategic significance for European citizens, rather than arcane agreements on process. Indeed, such appears to be one of the consequences of the crisis in Georgia.

The priority given by the French President to European defence, as one of the key building blocks of a more integrated and effective European Union, when taken together with the new strategic context in which the EU finds itself, constitutes the best prospect for serious progress for many years. It is clear that the French Presidency of the EU sought to launch a process that will evolve over the medium term and may well include, in addition to initiatives at the level of the Union, also an accord between smaller groups such as France and Britain for specific enhancements of military capability. If these are supported by real political will, they could truly lead to a stronger independent common defence capability within the EU open to all member states prepared to take on its goals and obligations. It is worth recalling, in this regard, that Sarkozy is likely to have a mandate even beyond 2012 and that in any event a strong ESDP is a shared view across the political spectrum in France.

However, whether this process will lead to further achievements also depends upon factors outside the EU. The outcome of the American presidential elections will certainly be of great significance. Though at a technical level, it already seems certain that both McCain and Obama would support a stronger European defence, the impact on European public opinion of an Obama Presidency for the image of the United States, though unclear, could be profound. After the relative engagement or isolationism of the next administration in Washington, the future actions of Moscow will also, plainly, have a decisive influence. So too will the existing or potential crises in the Middle East, particularly Afghanistan, Pakistan and Iran. All of this underlines the widespread perception that the European interest in achieving a more serious shared defence policy has remained still too reactive, an admission of common weakness rather than an ambition for concerted strength. But this sobering reality supports the underlining purpose of Sarkozy's strategy, which is to create a Europe that is less passive in the face of such influences and more the master of its own fate.

Notes

1   European Commission, *Eurobarometer* no. 66 and no. 68, December 2006 and December 2007. See also Jean-Dominique Giuliani, 'Comment relancer l'Europe de la défense?', *Défense nationale*, February 2008.

2   See The French National Assembly, in *Compte-rendu* no. 34, National Defence and Armed Forces Committee, 2006. http://www.assemblee-nationale.fr/12/cr-cdef/ 05-06/c0506034.asp

3   See Javier Solana, 'Where we Stand', in *The development of ESDP instruments during the German EU Presidency and beyond*, The Global Policy Institute, London, 2007.

4   As of December 2007, some 154,000 American soldiers were deployed in Iraq and as of May 2008 some 21,000 in Afghanistan with still an open-ended timescale on both commitments.

5   Speech by French President, Nicolas Sarkozy, before the United

States of America's joint session of Congress, Washington DC, 7 November 2007. http://www.elysee.fr

6 See speech by Sarkozy to the 15th Ambassadors' conference, Paris, 27 August 2007. http://www.elysee.fr

7 Ibid.

8 This followed the American decision to move toward a strategic graduated response in the nuclear balance with the former USSR. This move included the acceptance that a limited conflict involving only tactical nuclear weapons could unfold in Central Europe, a view diametrically opposed to the French concept governing nuclear deterrence of an immediate strategic response. Since this defence concept was coupled with the employment of conventional forces with nuclear forces, France withdrew from NATO's permanent military structure. See Jean-Pierre Maulny, 'Behind the politics of France's relationship to NATO', IRIS, Paris, February 2008.

9 Albeit it has been controversial in France in some quarters.

10 See *Le Livre blanc, Défense et sécurité nationale*, Odile Jacob and La documentation française, Paris, p. 110, June 2008.

11 Ibid.

12 Such a prospect should be welcomed by many within the organisation not least on account of the financial burden Paris would be assuming since its full return within the command structure would entail some 900 or so French additional officers being posted in the Alliance.

13 NATO Prague Summit Declaration, paragraph 3, 21 November 2002. See also Ray Henault, 'NATO in the 21st century', *Military Technology*, March 2006.

14 'France's defence review', *The Economist*, 19 June 2008.

15 She also gave a similar speech in Paris a few days before (on 22 February 2008).

16 See speech by the US Ambassador to NATO, Victoria Nuland, London, 25 February 2008. http://www.usembassy.org.uk/events/2008/2008_007.html.

17 See 'France's vision of defence is impaired', *Financial Times*, 22 June 2008.

18 Since 2002, French forces have been involved in Afghanistan, mainly in Kabul and in the regions of Kandahar and Jalalabad where the special forces have been deployed with to date some 1,700 French troops participating in the stabilisation of the country. See also http://www.rpfrance-otan.org/article.php3?id_article=581.

19 See Henri Bentégeat, 'The steps needed to move ESDP from theory to fact', *Europe's World*, Summer 2008.

20 Ibid.

21 See also Paul Cornish, 'EU and NATO: Cooperation or competition?', *Briefing paper, Policy department external policies*, European Parliament, October 2006.

22 Partly this derives from Ankara's negotiating strategy to advance Turkey's candidacy for EU membership. Partly it has been because Cyprus, one of the non-NATO EU Member States, does not have an agreement with the Alliance on protecting classified information and is not, unlike four other EU neutral countries (namely Austria, Ireland, Finland and Sweden), a member of NATO's Partnership for Peace Programme.

23 See Giuliani, loc. cit.

24 See speech by Sarkozy to the 15th Ambassadors' conference, loc. cit.

25 See speech by Miliband, College of Europe, Bruges, 15 November 2007. http://www.fco.gov.uk/en/newsroom/latest-news/speeches/

26 The EU operations centre has been ready for activation since January 2007. At present for a so-called autonomous action the EU has the option to make use of the facilities provided by any of the five national Operation Headquarters currently available in

the EU (in France, Britain, Germany, Greece and Italy).

27 See The Council of the European Union, *European security strategy, A secure Europe in a better world*, Brussels, December 2003.

28 Each battlegroup consists of 1,500 rapidly deployable troops. The missions envisaged include the activities required by the European security strategy as well as by the so-called 1992 Petersberg tasks, which encompass humanitarian and rescue tasks, peace-keeping tasks and tasks of combat forces in crisis management including peacemaking.

29 See Bentégeat, loc. cit.

30 Fotios Moustakis and Petros Violakis, *An Examination of the European Security and Defence Policy: Obstacles and Options*, Conflict Studies Research Centre, 06/40, Defence Academy of the United Kindgom, August 2006, p. 5.

31 See European Defence Agency, 'European-United States defence expenditures 2006', December 2007.

32 See European Commission, 'A strategy for a stronger and more competitive European defence industry', COM (2007) 764 final, Brussels, December 2007.

33 See Stephen Haseler and Jeannette Ladzik, *The development of ESDP instruments during the German EU Presidency and beyond*, The Global Policy Institute, 2007, p. 69.

34 See Yves Fromion, 'Industrie d'armement terrestre européenne et présidence française de l'UE', *Défense nationale*, Eurosatory, p. 31, June 2008; and in 'Rapport sur les moyens de structurer et de développer une industrie européenne de défense', 17 July 2008. http://www.defense.gouv.fr/europe_de_la_defense

35 See European Commission, 'Intra-Community transfer of defence products', 2005. http://ec.europa.eu/enterprise/regulation/inst_sp/defense_en.htm

36 The 1998 Letter of Intent signed by six Member States, the so-called LoI states, followed by the Farnborough agreement in 2000, sought to provide an improvement to this by facilitating the restructuring of the European defence industry via *inter alia* common measures on simplified export procedures. See European Commission, 'Proposal for a directive of the European parliament and of the Council on simplifying terms and conditions of transfers defence-related products within the Community', COM (2007) 765 final, Brussels, December 2007.

37 Ibid.

38 See European Defence Agency, Press release, April 2008. The 26 EU member states who are part of the European Defence Agency further endorsed on 8 July 2008 a Capability Development Plan for future military needs and priorities for the European Security and Defence Policy. This was developed jointly by the European Defence Agency, the EU military committee, the EU Council General Secretariat and the member states.

39 See: Strategic dossier, *European military capabilities: Building armed forces for modern operations*, International Institute for Strategic Studies, London, July 2008, p. 154.

40 At a national level, it had significantly led in particular to preparations for the 1996 decision to build up a more substantial force projection capability.

41 See *Le Livre blanc, Défense et sécurité nationale*, op. cit., pp. 44 and 213.

42 This might entail, in particular, a greater cooperation on a bilateral basis with Britain.

43 See François Heisbourg, 'Knowledge holds the key to French defence', *Financial Times*, 18 June 2008.

44 See *Le Livre blanc, Défense et sécurité nationale*, op. cit., p. 81.

45 Ibid, chapter 4 and p. 266.

46 Through the Airbus multi-purpose aircraft programme.

47 The difficulties encountered in ensuring the availability of the assets for the recent ESDP operation in Chad are telling evidence concerning such a need.

48 Article 28A (6) of the Treaty of Lisbon allows 'those Member States whose military capabilities fulfil higher criteria and which have made more binding commitments to one another in this area' to participate to the PSC framework.

49 'Miliband backs strong EU military force', *The Guardian*, 2 July 2008.

50 See speech by Sarkozy on defence and national security, Paris, 17 June 2008. http://www.elysee.fr

51 See Lasserre Isabelle, 'Les ambitieux projets de Paris pour la défense européenne', *Le Figaro*, 26 June 2008.

52 See speech by the French Minister for Foreign Affairs, Bernard Kouchner, at the EU-NATO High Level seminar, Paris, 7 July 2008. http://www.diplomatie.gouv.fr

53 See speech by Sarkozy, at the opening of the 16th Ambassador's conference, Paris, 27 August 2008. http://www.elysee.fr

54 This examination was agreed upon at the December 2007 European Council. See Presidency conclusions, *Brussels European Council 14 December 2007*, 16616/1/07, The Council of the European Union, 14 February 2008.

55 The first British national security strategy statement asserts that Britain 'will work for a stronger and more accountable European foreign and security policy'. See *The National strategy of the United Kingdom: Security in an interdependent world*, Cabinet Office, London, March 2008.

56 Joint UK-France Summit Declaration, 28 March 2008. http://www.pm.gov.uk/files/pdf/UK-FR%20Communique%20270308.pdf

57 This target aims at improving the EU's civilian capability to respond effectively to crisis management tasks and at ensuring that the EU can conduct these in line with the European Security Strategy and with the support functions and equipment required. See 'Civilian headline goal 2010', doc. 14823/07, European Council, 19 November 2007.

58 See speech by Miliband to the think-tank Progress, House of Commons, London, 2 July 2008. http://www.fco.gov.uk/en/newsroom/latest-news/speeches/

59 See Prime Minister Gordon Brown in *Le Monde*, 'Une Europe mondiale peut changer les choses', 26 March 2008.

60 See Alastair Cameron, 'The Upcoming French Presidency of the European Union', *Newsbrief*, Royal United Services Institute, London, 15 May 2008.

61 See Valasek Tomas, 'France, NATO and European Defence', *Policy Brief*, Centre for European Reform, 12 May 2008.

62 See Kamp Karl-Heinz, *After the Summit: Long-Term consequences for NATO*, Research Paper no. 37, NATO Defence College, May 2008.